NFL TODAY

THE STORY OF THE
NEW YORK GIANTS

NFL TODAY

THE STORY OF THE NEW YORK GIANTS

MICHAEL E. GOODMAN

CREATIVE EDUCATION

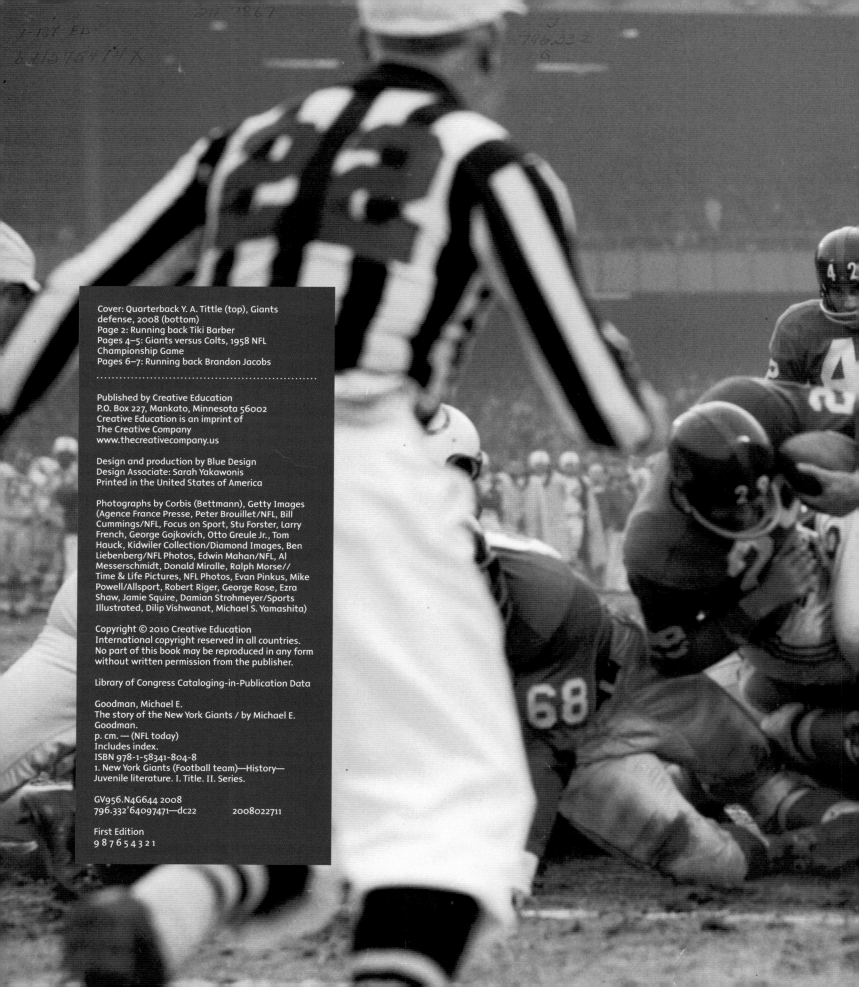

Cover: Quarterback Y. A. Tittle (top), Giants
defense, 2008 (bottom)
Page 2: Running back Tiki Barber
Pages 4–5: Giants versus Colts, 1958 NFL
Championship Game
Pages 6–7: Running back Brandon Jacobs

....

Published by Creative Education
P.O. Box 227, Mankato, Minnesota 56002
Creative Education is an imprint of
The Creative Company
www.thecreativecompany.us

Design and production by Blue Design
Design Associate: Sarah Yakawonis
Printed in the United States of America

Photographs by Corbis (Bettmann), Getty Images
(Agence France Presse, Peter Brouillet/NFL, Bill
Cummings/NFL, Focus on Sport, Stu Forster, Larry
French, George Gojkovich, Otto Greule Jr., Tom
Hauck, Kidwiler Collection/Diamond Images, Ben
Liebenberg/NFL Photos, Edwin Mahan/NFL, Al
Messerschmidt, Donald Miralle, Ralph Morse//
Time & Life Pictures, NFL Photos, Evan Pinkus, Mike
Powell/Allsport, Robert Riger, George Rose, Ezra
Shaw, Jamie Squire, Damian Strohmeyer/Sports
Illustrated, Dilip Vishwanat, Michael S. Yamashita)

Library of Congress Cataloging-in-Publication Data

Goodman, Michael E.
The story of the New York Giants / by Michael E.
Goodman.
p. cm. — (NFL today)
Includes index.
ISBN 978-1-58341-804-8
1. New York Giants (Football team)—History—
Juvenile literature. I. Title. II. Series.

GV956.N4G644 2008
796.332'64097471—dc22   2008022711

First Edition
9 8 7 6 5 4 3 2 1

CONTENTS

SMALL INVESTMENT, GIANT RETURN 8

GIFFORD AND THE GOLDEN AGE 16

SIMMS LEADS A SUPER TURNAROUND 22

ON THE FAST TRACK WITH FASSEL 30

ELI EMERGES 38

INDEX 48

ON THE SIDELINES

SNEAKING TO VICTORY 12

SUMMERALL'S SNOWY SCORE 20

MIRACLE OF THE MEADOWLANDS. 27

DUNK YOU VERY MUCH 35

COACH FASSEL'S GUARANTEE. 41

THE DRIVE. 42

MEET THE GIANTS

TIM MARA 11

MEL HEIN 15

FRANK GIFFORD 24

LAWRENCE TAYLOR 32

PHIL SIMMS 36

BILL PARCELLS 46

SMALL INVESTMENT,
GIANT RETURN

There is an old saying that America's largest city is so big and important that they named it twice—New York, New York. The first capital of the United States and still the center of business and culture in the country, New York is the home of many of the nation's major financial institutions, largest theaters and museums, and most expensive restaurants. Nowhere in the country will a person find larger crowds, longer traffic jams, or noisier sports fans.

Since 1925, many of the loudest fans have been those cheering for the New York Giants of the National Football League (NFL). The team played its first games in the Polo Grounds, the stadium that major league baseball's New York Giants called home. So the team's first owner called his club the Giants, too. The baseball Giants moved to San Francisco long ago, but the football team affectionately known as the "Jints" has stayed in the New York metropolitan area for more than 80 years and has built one of the most loyal fan bases in American sports.

In 1925, a New York businessman and sports promoter named Tim Mara wanted to buy a partial interest in a top professional boxer named Gene Tunney. When his bid was turned down, Mara decided to buy a franchise in the new NFL instead for the bargain rate of $500. At the time, football was

X New York City is home to some of America's most famous buildings, bridges, statues, and sports franchises—it is the only city to feature two NFL teams (Giants and Jets).

mainly a college sport, and pro football teams were based primarily in the Midwest. No one knew if a pro team would attract fans and make money in New York. But the price tag for the club seemed too good for Mara to pass up. "I figured that even an empty store in New York City was worth more than $500," he said.

The franchise took a while to begin making money, however. During the 1925 season, Mara and his two young sons (ages 17 and 9), who made up the team's entire staff, gave away almost as many tickets as they sold just so the stands wouldn't be empty. The Giants started out 0–3 and then found the winning touch. Behind running backs Jack McBride and Henry "Hinkey" Haines, the club finished its first campaign with an 8–4 record.

Over the next few years, the Giants continued to improve on the field but to fare poorly at the ticket office. Mara may have been losing money, but he was thrilled when the club earned its first NFL title in 1927 by posting a league-best 11–1–1 record. That championship team featured an outstanding defense that recorded a remarkable 10 shutouts and gave up only 20 points all season. Anchoring the defense were three giant-sized tackles (each weighed nearly 250 pounds) and future Hall-of-Famers—Pete Henry, Cal Hubbard, and Steve Owen.

TIM MARA

TEAM FOUNDER, OWNER
GIANTS SEASONS: 1925-59

In 1925, Tim Mara was probably the only man in New York City with the daring and imagination to make pro football a success in "The Big Apple." Sports fans in New York loved college football but had a low opinion of the professional variety. Getting them to buy tickets to pro games required a master salesman, and that's what Mara was. "The man was a promotional genius," said local businessman Toots Shor. "You could tell him he had to make germs the most popular thing in town, and he'd find a way. Soon, he'd get everybody in New York absolutely nuts to have germs on their block." But getting people excited about attending Giants games was almost as tough. It would take several years before the team turned a profit, and Mara's $500 initial investment would balloon to well over $25,000 with expenses for players' salaries, stadium rental, program printing, uniforms, and equipment. Still, he persevered because he believed in the Giants and saw the team as his family's gift to New York. Mara's descendants still own and manage the franchise today.

ON THE SIDELINES

SNEAKING TO VICTORY

When the Giants took on the Chicago Bears in the 1934 NFL Championship Game, they were really battling two opponents: the Bears and the ice-covered field of the Polo Grounds. Following four days of rain and a sudden drop in temperature to 0 °F, the field was nearly as slippery as a hockey rink. Giants captain and end Ray Flaherty suggested that his teammates trade in their football cleats for sneakers, and an equipment manager was sent to a nearby college to bring back as many pairs of basketball shoes as he could find. He returned by halftime, with the Giants trailing 10–3. The players donned the sneakers and returned to the field for the second half. When Bears coach George Halas noticed the shoe change, he told his players to step on the Giants' toes. But the suddenly sure-footed Jints easily outran their opponents and raced to a 30–13 victory to capture their second league title. "The effect of the new footwear was magical," wrote one New York reporter. The 1934 title contest has gone down in NFL history as "The Sneakers Game."

In 1931, Mara appointed Owen as player-coach and gave him a long-term contract. Owen would remain the Giants' head coach for the next 23 years. The club also outbid two other teams for the services of versatile lineman Mel Hein from Washington State University by offering him $150 a game. Hein played every minute of every Giants game for the next 15 years, serving as both center on offense and linebacker on defense. "And in all that time, I can count on the fingers of one hand the mistakes he made offensively and defensively," said Coach Owen.

Led by Hein, halfback Ed Danowski, and two-way back Alphonse "Tuffy" Leemans, Owen's teams were the dominant force of the NFL's Eastern Division during the 1930s and '40s. They captured nine division titles between 1933 and 1946 and took home two NFL championship trophies in 1934 and 1938.

In the late 1940s, the Giants began to show their age and slipped in the standings. New York fans were shocked in 1947 and 1948 when the club posted back-to-back losing seasons for the first time in its history. The team returned to its winning ways in the early 1950s, led by quarterback Charlie Conerly, who quickly began setting team passing records. But the Giants consistently finished behind the Cleveland Browns in their conference from 1951 through 1955 and did not reach the postseason again until 1956. By that time, Coach Owen had retired and been replaced by former Giants end Jim Lee Howell, who took on the task of building another championship-caliber team.

Charlie Conerly was an icon of manliness in the 1950s, a former Marine who led the Giants to an NFL title and acted as the "Marlboro Man" in cigarette commercials. **✕**

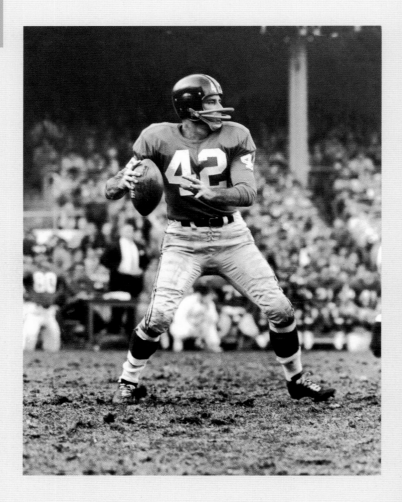

MEL HEIN

CENTER, LINEBACKER
GIANTS SEASONS: 1931-45
HEIGHT: 6-FOOT-2
WEIGHT: 225 POUNDS

Mel Hein was one of pro football's first great all-around players. An unmovable blocker at center on offense and a devastating tackler at linebacker on defense, Hein was on the field for 60 minutes of every game during his 15-year career with the Giants. "He was impervious to injuries. I heard him call an injury timeout only once and that was late in his career when he was kicked in the nose in a pileup by one of our own players," said former Giants owner Wellington Mara. Although not much bigger than average in size, Hein was strong and tough. Defenders who attempted to bull past him when the Giants had the ball often found themselves flat on the ground, thanks to a strong block or a well-placed forearm shiver. On defense, Hein pioneered new methods for covering passes and jamming receivers at the line of scrimmage. During the 10 seasons Hein served as team captain, the Giants played in 7 league championship games and won 2 titles. A five-time All-Pro, Hein was in the first class elected to the Pro Football Hall of Fame in 1963.

[15]

GIFFORD AND THE GOLDEN AGE

When Coach Howell took over, he inherited a solid nucleus
that included Conerly, running back Frank Gifford, and
offensive tackle Roosevelt Brown. He then engineered trades
for fullback Alex Webster and defensive end Andy Robustelli
and drafted linebacker Sam Huff. These players formed the
core of the Giants team that celebrated its move to Yankee
Stadium in 1956 by winning the NFL championship.

Gifford, who starred in that championship game victory
over the Chicago Bears, was named the NFL's Player of the
Year in 1956. The talented Californian with movie-star looks
was the team's top scorer, runner, and pass receiver that
season. "Frank was the body and soul of our team," said
Coach Howell. "He was the player we went to in the clutch."

Two years later, Gifford led the Giants back to another
NFL title game. This time, New York battled the Baltimore Colts
in a contest that has been called "The Greatest Game Ever
Played." The two clubs featured a combined total of 17 future
members of the Pro Football Hall of Fame, and their matchup

was promoted as an epic battle in the New York and national press. There was so much press coverage that more people tuned into the game on television than had ever watched a pro football game before.

The drama-packed contest was the first NFL Championship Game in which the outcome was decided in sudden-death overtime. Millions of viewers watched with rapt attention as the Colts tied the game late in the fourth quarter and eked out a 23–17 win six minutes into the extra session. From then on, pro football became the most popular televised sport in America. "We didn't know it at the time," recalled NFL commissioner Pete Rozelle, "but it was the beginning for the NFL. From that game forward, our fan base grew and grew. We owe both franchises a huge debt."

The Giants and Colts again faced off for the league championship following the 1959 season, with Baltimore staging a fourth-quarter comeback to once again end New York's title hopes. Then the Giants underwent a changing of the guard in the early 1960s, hoping to find the right championship combination. First, Howell retired and was replaced by assistant coach Allie Sherman. Sherman then revamped the club's offense by trading with the San Francisco 49ers for 35-year-old quarterback Y. A. Tittle. The 49ers

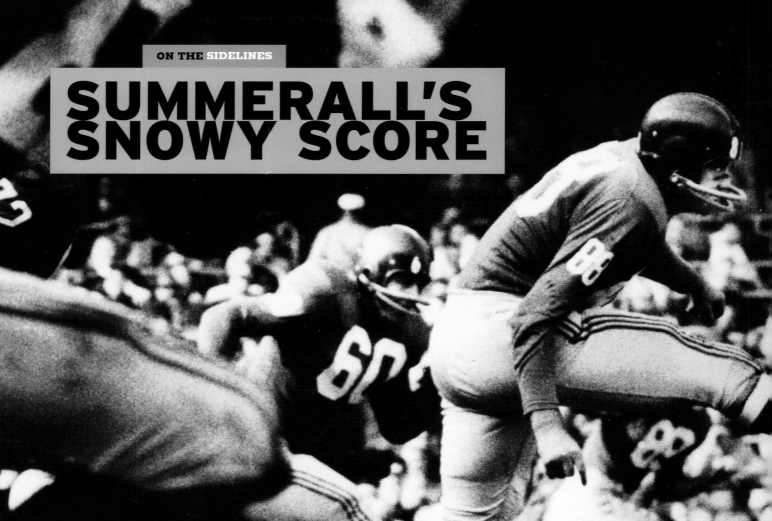

SUMMERALL'S SNOWY SCORE

In the last regular-season game of 1958, the Giants faced the Cleveland Browns in a driving snowstorm at Yankee Stadium, needing a win to force a playoff with the Browns for the division title. A tie or loss would put Cleveland into the NFL Championship Game against the Baltimore Colts. The teams skidded and pounded their way to a 10–10 tie late in the fourth quarter. With two minutes remaining, the Giants faced a 4th-down-and-10 situation somewhere across the 50-yard line. (No one could see the yard markers under the snow.) Coach Jim Lee Howell shocked nearly everyone by sending in kicker Pat Summerall to attempt a long field goal. "I couldn't believe Jim Lee was asking me to do that," recalled Summerall. "It was a bad field, and it was so unrealistic." But Summerall put his full foot into the kick—which started out wide to the left, then curved inside the uprights for the win. Thanks to Summerall's miraculous kick, the Giants were able to make NFL history two weeks later when they took on the Colts in "The Greatest Game Ever Played."

thought Tittle was past his prime, but he found a new lease on life in New York. "The Old Man" led the Giants to three straight Eastern Conference titles between 1961 and 1963, though the club came up short in the NFL Championship Game each time.

After the Giants lost their third straight title game in 1963, they fell apart quickly. Several stars were traded away, while others, such as Gifford and Tittle, soon retired. The club won just two games in 1964 and only one in 1966 and found itself in an unfamiliar place—the cellar of the Eastern Conference. Throughout the rest of the 1960s and '70s, the Giants shuffled through four coaches and five starting quarterbacks, played in four different stadiums, and put together just two winning seasons.

The Jints featured several outstanding offensive players during those down years, including scrambling quarterback Fran Tarkenton, tight end Bob Tucker, and running back Rob Johnson. Yet the club's defense was in shambles. The offense could not put up enough points to offset what the defense gave up each game. New York fans began wondering if they would ever cheer for a winner again.

SIMMS LEADS A SUPER TURNAROUND

To add to the turmoil the franchise was undergoing in the early 1970s, the Giants found themselves homeless in 1973 when the Yankees decided to renovate Yankee Stadium and use it for baseball only. So, the Giants began building their own stadium in the Meadowlands in nearby New Jersey. While the stadium was under construction, they played home games 80 miles from New York at the Yale Bowl in New Haven, Connecticut, for two years and shared Shea Stadium with the New York Jets in 1975. Changing locations didn't change the team's bad luck, however. Even when the club finally moved into Giants Stadium in 1976, it continued to struggle.

The Giants' prospects began to improve when George Young came on board in 1979 as the team's general manager. Young's reputation for having built successful NFL teams in both Baltimore and Miami preceded him. But Giants fans questioned his first big move: selecting Phil Simms, an unknown quarterback from Morehead State University in

Although quarterback Phil Simms wasn't particularly great at anything—he never led the NFL in passing yards, accuracy, or touchdowns—he was well-rounded, with very few weaknesses. X

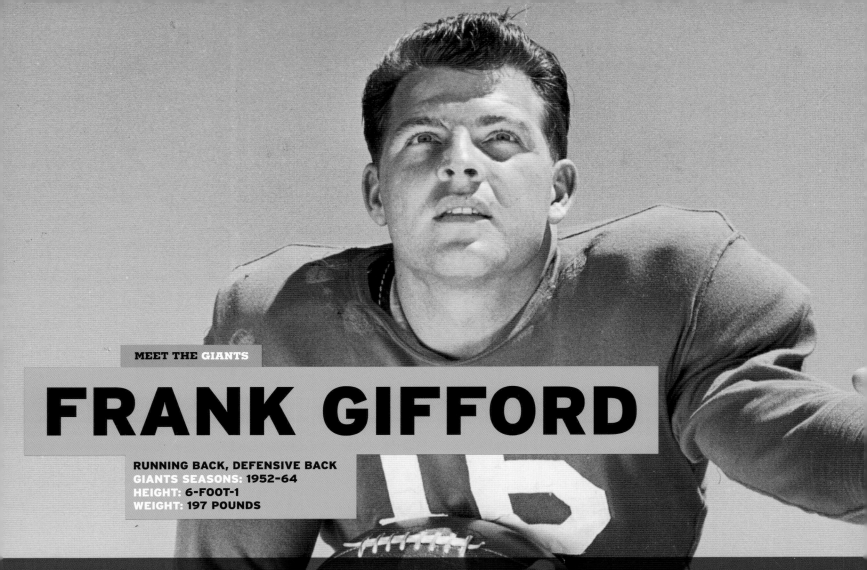

FRANK GIFFORD

RUNNING BACK, DEFENSIVE BACK
GIANTS SEASONS: 1952–64
HEIGHT: 6-FOOT-1
WEIGHT: 197 POUNDS

Frank Gifford had it all—great looks; a powerful body; an outgoing personality; and outstanding talent as a runner, passer, pass receiver, and defensive back. "Frank lent a certain dignity and tone to our entire organization," said team owner Jack Mara. The Giants' top draft pick in 1952, Gifford would impress New York fans with his all-around great play for more than a decade and still holds the team record for touchdowns scored (78). Gifford's best year came in 1956, when he was named the NFL's Most Valuable Player (MVP) while leading the Giants to their first NFL title in 18 years. That year, Gifford ranked fifth in the league in rushing and third in pass receiving, threw two touchdown passes, and scored nine other touchdowns. Although not a fast runner, Gifford could quickly spot any opening in the defense and burst through the hole with amazing speed. He played in eight Pro Bowls and was inducted into the Pro Football Hall of Fame in 1977. Following his football career, Gifford remained in the public spotlight as a television sports commentator and program host.

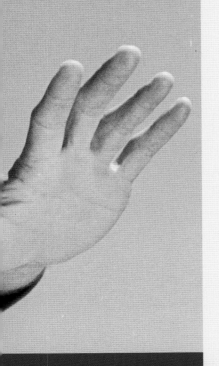

Kentucky, as the team's top pick in the 1979 NFL Draft. The next day, newspaper headlines in several New York City area papers read: "Phil Who?"

During the next 15 seasons, New Yorkers came to appreciate Simms for his talent, courage, and ability to perform in the clutch. Before the star quarterback retired, he would set nearly every Giants passing record. Simms's arrival in New York signaled the start of the franchise's return to respectability. But it was Young's top draft choice in 1981—linebacker Lawrence Taylor—who really transformed the Giants into one of the NFL's most exciting and feared teams.

Taylor was a special player who helped revolutionize the position of outside linebacker with his speed, anticipation, and aggressiveness. "The ability he had—I still think back to how amazing it was to watch him on film," said fellow linebacker Brad Van Pelt. "He was actually stepping right with the snap of the ball. While everybody else was still at a standstill, he was moving toward the ball—that's amazing."

Playing under new head coach Bill Parcells, Simms directed the offense, and Taylor headed up the defense that propelled the Giants into the playoffs in 1984 and 1985. The Jints were even better in 1986, finishing with a 14–2 record. Taylor was named the NFL's MVP that year, and running back Joe Morris

and tight end Mark Bavaro emerged as offensive stars.

In the postseason, the Giants crushed the San Francisco 49ers and Washington Redskins to reach Super Bowl XXI in January 1987 against the Denver Broncos. Simms's performance was outstanding in the title game. He completed a remarkable 22 of 25 passes (a Super Bowl-record 88 percent) to lead New York to a 39–20 victory and its first NFL championship in 30 years.

Coach Parcells's crew made another championship drive in 1990. With running back Ottis Anderson taking handoffs from Simms and following his massive blockers, the Jints ground down their opponents that year. They started out the season with 10 straight victories. Then, after dropping two of the next three games, the team suffered an even greater loss when Simms went down with a season-ending foot injury.

Backup quarterback Jeff Hostetler led the Giants to victories in their last two regular-season games. Then the team's defense took over in the playoffs, as the Giants dominated Chicago and San Francisco to earn a berth in Super Bowl XXV against the Buffalo Bills.

Using their running game to perfection, the Giants controlled the ball and the clock for almost the entire Super

MIRACLE AT THE MEADOWLANDS

The Giants lost many more games than they won in the 1970s, but no loss was more devastating than the one to the rival Philadelphia Eagles in November 1978. Amazingly, that terrible loss proved to be the impetus for turning the team around. With just 30 seconds left in the game, the Giants were leading the Eagles 17–12. Quarterback Joe Pisarcik needed only to take a knee to run out the clock and break the team's latest losing streak. But that isn't what happened. Instead, the Giants' offensive coordinator sent in a play calling for a handoff to running back Larry Csonka. Pisarcik took the snap and reached the ball out toward Csonka—too low. It glanced off Csonka's knee for a fumble that was scooped up by Eagles defensive back Herman Edwards and returned for a Philly touchdown and a 19–17 win. New York sportswriters sarcastically began calling the play the "Miracle at the Meadowlands." After the loss, several Giants coaches were fired, and a shakeup began in New York that eventually led the Giants back to the top of the NFL.

X After having thrown only 58 total passes in his first 4 NFL seasons, quarterback Jeff Hostetler (pictured) helped the Giants find Super Bowl glory when Phil Simms was injured in 1990.

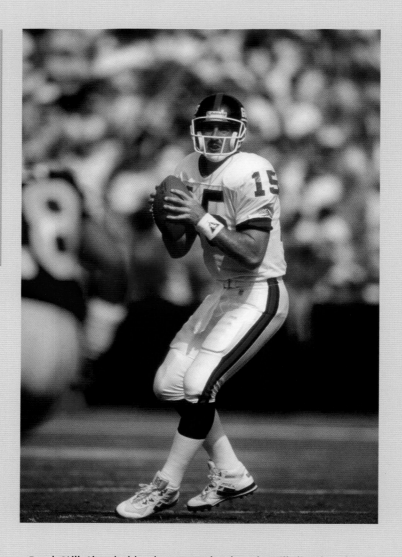

Bowl. Still, they held only a 20–19 lead as the Bills lined up for a potential game-winning field goal in the closing seconds. When the kick by Buffalo's Scott Norwood sailed wide right of the uprights, the Giants claimed their sixth NFL championship.

Although he was 33 years old and in the twilight of his NFL career, Ottis Anderson had a big game in Super Bowl XXV, piling up 102 rushing yards for the victorious Giants. X

ON THE FAST TRACK WITH FASSEL

x --------

The club went into a decline in the early 1990s as, one by one, the team's former stars suffered career-altering injuries or moved on. When both Simms and Taylor hung up their Giants jerseys at the end of the 1993 season, fans knew that another golden era had ended.

After going just 6–10 in 1996, the Giants hired offensive specialist Jim Fassel as their new head coach. Fassel's first squad got off to a 1–3 start, and fans in Giants Stadium booed loudly. But Fassel refused to make drastic changes. "The little red panic button is always there if you want to reach up and push it," he said. "But I would have lost them right then if I started to make wholesale changes…. Everything I had told them about being consistent and staying the course would have gone out the window."

The boos quickly turned to cheers as Fassel's new offensive system began to click. Led by quarterback Danny Kanell, the team finished the 1997 season 10–5–1. In just one year, Coach Fassel had helped lift the team from last place to first in the National Football Conference (NFC) East Division.

Fassel's Giants kept winning and, by 2000, were ready for another championship run. Behind strong-armed quarterback Kerry Collins and elusive running back Tiki Barber on offense and overpowering end Michael Strahan on defense, the

X Even though the Giants were often a mediocre team in the mid-1990s, players such as defensive lineman Keith Hamilton helped maintain New York's tradition of physical defense.

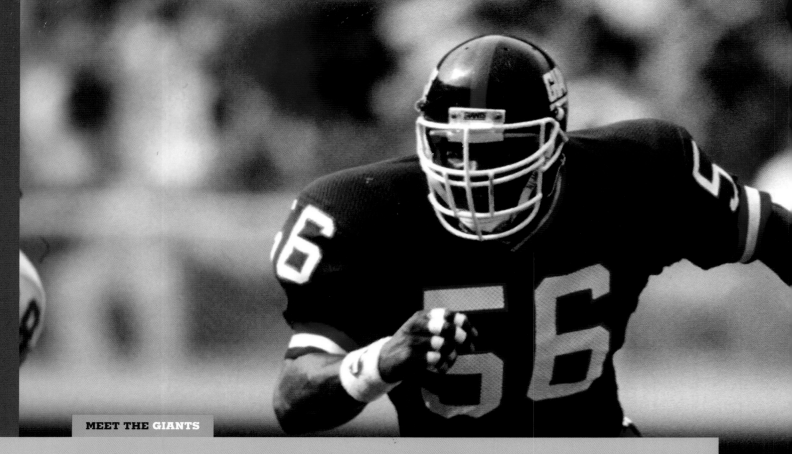

LAWRENCE TAYLOR

LINEBACKER
GIANTS SEASONS: 1981-93
HEIGHT: 6-FOOT-3
WEIGHT: 240 POUNDS

No defensive player has ever disrupted an opponent's offense more completely than Lawrence Taylor. When "L. T." lined up at his outside linebacker position, poised to charge the quarterback or take on a receiver, linemen forgot counts and often jumped offsides. Quarterbacks fidgeted nervously and dropped back quicker than usual, hoping to avoid a sack. Even when he was triple-teamed by blockers, Taylor often found a way to break up the play. "If there was ever a Superman in the NFL," said former Washington Redskins quarterback Joe Theismann, "I think he wore number 56 for the Giants." Taylor had not only great talent but also an intense work ethic. "Lawrence Taylor brought energy to the team, in games and in practice, and it rubbed off on all the other guys," said teammate Phil Simms. "Players around him would say, 'Hey, I got to try harder, otherwise I'll look absolutely horrific out there playing next to Lawrence Taylor.'" L. T. was a Pro Bowl selection for 10 consecutive years and was named league MVP in 1986. He was inducted into the Hall of Fame in 1999.

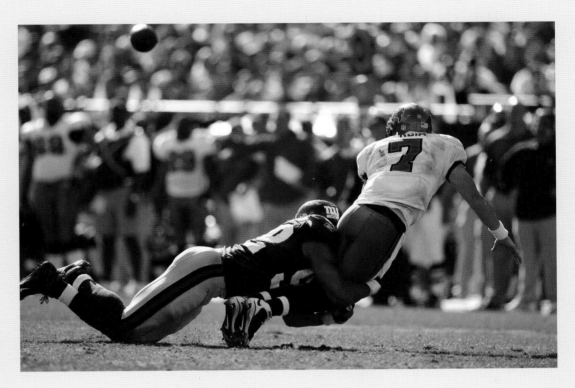

Giants finished the 2000 season with five straight victories to capture another division title. Barber recorded the first of his six 1,000-yard rushing seasons with the Giants, while Strahan built on his reputation as one of the league's best at sacking the quarterback.

The Jints added two more wins in the playoffs to capture the NFC crown and reach the Super Bowl against the Baltimore Ravens. However, New York's exciting run stopped there, as the fierce Ravens defense shut down the Giants 34–7.

X Michael Strahan enjoyed numerous All-Pro seasons, but 2001 was truly the season of a lifetime, as he set a new NFL record with 22.5 sacks.

Before entering the NFL, tight end Jeremy Shockey helped the powerhouse University of Miami Hurricanes win college football's 2001 national championship.

In the 2002 NFL Draft, the Giants added 6-foot-5 and 255-pound tight end Jeremy Shockey to their offensive arsenal. The rookie was an instant star, leading all NFL tight ends in receptions (74) and receiving yards (894). Known for his fiery personality, he was also the league's "trash-talking" leader. Shockey's ability to catch passes and carry defenders on his back for big gains forced opponents to double-team him, which helped open up the field for other Giants receivers

DUNK YOU VERY MUCH

The Giants won 17 games during their magical 1986 season, including the Super Bowl. After each victory, linebacker Harry Carson would celebrate by dumping a full bucket of sports drink and ice over the head of coach Bill Parcells. It started a tradition that even high school and college sports teams have since adopted. "The reason I had to keep doing it," recalled Carson, "was that Bill was superstitious. If you do something and it works, you keep doing it. We were winning, so I kept giving him the shower." Actually, Carson was not the first Giants player to dunk the coach. Nose tackle Jim Burt started the practice in 1985—and not to celebrate. He was angry that Parcells had been on his back all week during practice before a big game against the Washington Redskins. After the Giants won the game, Burt got his revenge by soaking Parcells. The dunking cooled off any bad feelings between the two men. When Carson started showering the coach the next year, it created a close bond that helped the team win a championship.

[35]

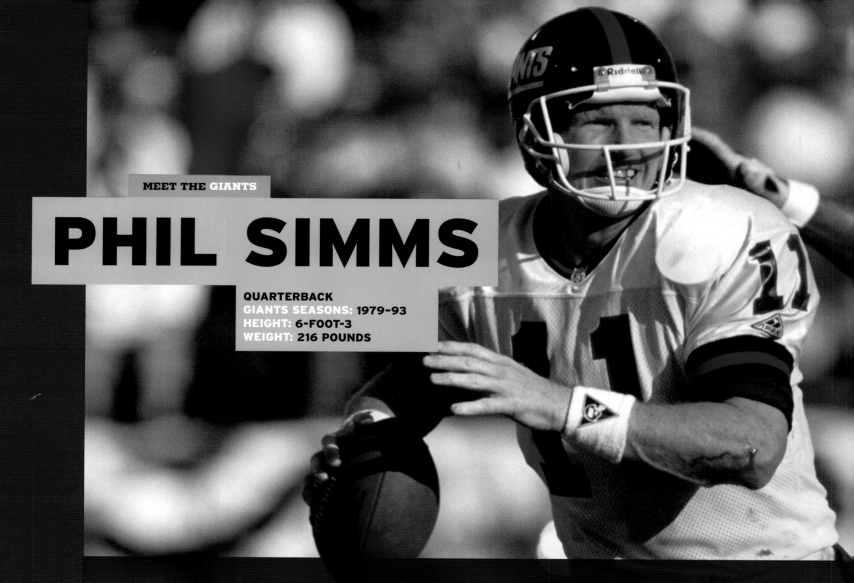

PHIL SIMMS

QUARTERBACK
GIANTS SEASONS: 1979–93
HEIGHT: 6-FOOT-3
WEIGHT: 216 POUNDS

When Phil Simms joined the Giants as a surprise first-round draft pick in 1979, the team had endured 6 straight losing seasons and had not appeared in a postseason game in 15 years. The losing continued during Simms's first five seasons in New York, as he suffered through growing pains learning how to be an NFL quarterback and real pains from a variety of terrible injuries. Then, beginning in 1984, Simms took full control of the team's offense, leading the Giants to three straight playoff berths and finally a Super Bowl championship in 1986, earning MVP honors. "Phil Simms started to show us his confidence—the way he carried himself in the locker room, the way he carried himself on the field," said Giants linebacker Lawrence Taylor, "and we all became confident that he was going to get the job done." Known for his fiery, competitive spirit, Simms played all 15 of his pro seasons in New York and still holds more than half of the team's passing records. His number 11 jersey was retired in 1995.

such as speedsters Ike Hilliard and Amani Toomer. The result was a 10–6 record and another trip to the playoffs.

The 2003 season turned out to be a mixed blessing in New York. On the negative side, the Giants played poorly for most of the year, finishing last in their division and costing Coach Fassel his job. He was replaced by Tom Coughlin, a former Giants assistant under Bill Parcells. On the positive side, the Giants' poor record "earned" them the fourth pick in the NFL Draft. They traded that selection and several other draft choices to the San Diego Chargers for the chance to obtain the top pick in the draft, quarterback Eli Manning from the University of Mississippi.

Manning, whose father Archie and brother Peyton were also star NFL quarterbacks, arrived in New York with great fanfare. "Eli's Coming," headlines read in New York papers, echoing the title of a hit song from the late 1960s. Giants fans hoped that championships would also soon be coming to New York now that Manning was there.

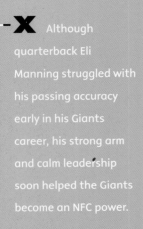

X Although quarterback Eli Manning struggled with his passing accuracy early in his Giants career, his strong arm and calm leadership soon helped the Giants become an NFC power.

Coach Coughlin's original plan for Manning was to let him watch from the sidelines his first year, observing veteran quarterback Kurt Warner. But when the Giants began struggling in midseason, Manning was thrown into the starting role. Nervous and inexperienced, the rookie made a lot of mistakes that year.

Manning was labeled as "inconsistent" during his next two seasons in New York as well. "He throws off of the wrong foot," some football experts said. "He doesn't read defenses well and rushes his passes," others noted. But nearly everyone believed he had a special talent that would eventually emerge. "He makes decisive decisions ... and he gets rid of the ball. You love to see that in a young quarterback," said Hall of Fame quarterback Dan Marino.

Manning weathered the criticism and began asserting his leadership on the field, especially in late-game, clutch situations. Behind his passing and the outstanding running and receiving of All-Pro Tiki Barber, the Giants reached the playoffs in both 2005 and 2006. But they failed to win a playoff contest either year.

Giants fans were nervous as the 2007 season began. Barber had retired, and the offensive burden now fell more squarely onto Manning's shoulders. When the team lost its first two games badly and barely won its third, fans were certain that 2007 would be a lost season in New York. Then the club rebounded, finishing the season at 10–6, good enough to claim a Wild Card berth in the playoffs.

That was only the beginning. During the Giants' first three postseason games, Manning displayed a confidence he had never shown before in his career. Alternating passes to receivers such as Plaxico Burress and Amani Toomer and handoffs to running backs Brandon Jacobs and Ahmad Bradshaw, Manning directed a Giants offense that suddenly seemed unstoppable. The high point was the NFC Championship Game, in which Manning outplayed future Hall-of-Famer Brett Favre of the Green Bay Packers at frigid Lambeau Field to lead the Giants to Super Bowl XLII.

The Giants went into the Super Bowl as heavy underdogs to the New England Patriots, who had won all 16 of their regular-season games, plus 2 playoff games, and were determined to become the first NFL team to go 19–0 in

COACH FASSEL'S GUARANTEE

During the first half of the 2000 season, the Giants surprised many experts by storming out to a 7–2 record. Then they badly lost two consecutive games at home and looked lifeless in both defeats. Coach Jim Fassel foresaw the season slipping away unless the team underwent a dramatic change. Fassel, who was not known for delivering fiery speeches, called a press conference and, putting his own job on the line, issued a guarantee: "Get off my coaches' and players' backs. I'm taking full responsibility right now," he declared. "I'm not afraid to say one thing—we're going to the playoffs." Fassel's announcement made headlines in New York and stirred up the team's locker room. "It even shocked us, the players, that our coach would stick his neck out so far," said All-Pro defensive end Michael Strahan. "We all got caught up in the positive spirit." The Giants won all five of their remaining regular-season games and kept winning in the playoffs, going all the way to Super Bowl XXXV before finally losing to the Baltimore Ravens.

THE DRIVE

During the first 41 Super Bowls, only one game had ever featured a successful last-minute, come-from-behind touchdown drive. So history was not on quarterback Eli Manning's side when he led the Giants' offense onto the field in the last three minutes of Super Bowl XLII in February 2008, trailing the New England Patriots 14–10. The Giants made two first downs, then the drive nearly stalled out. On a tense fourth-down-and-one play, halfback Brandon Jacobs bulled through Patriots defenders for a crucial first down. Three plays later, Manning narrowly avoided being sacked and heaved a 32-yard pass to receiver David Tyree, who pinned the ball against his helmet and somehow hung on to it for dear life. Giants players on the sidelines were now certain that their team would win and began chanting, "17–14" to each other, predicting the final score. Four plays later, their prediction became reality when Manning connected with receiver Plaxico Burress for the winning touchdown. For days, New York sportswriters and fans debated what to name the Giants' amazing victory charge, then decided to call it simply "The Drive."

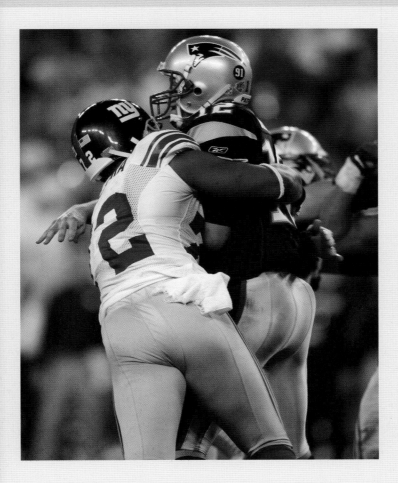

a season. But the Jints unveiled an aggressive, blitzing defense led by Strahan and fellow defensive end Osi Umenyiora that held the high-powered Patriots offense in check into the fourth quarter.

Even after New England took a 14–10 lead with less than three minutes remaining, the Giants weren't ready to concede the championship. Manning directed a scoring drive that featured perhaps the most exciting play in Super Bowl history—he ducked and spun his way out of the grasp of several tacklers and then completed a long pass to wide receiver David Tyree to keep the drive alive. Then Manning

X Playing and learning alongside Michael Strahan, defensive end Osi Umenyiora (pictured) became a feared pass rusher in his own right.

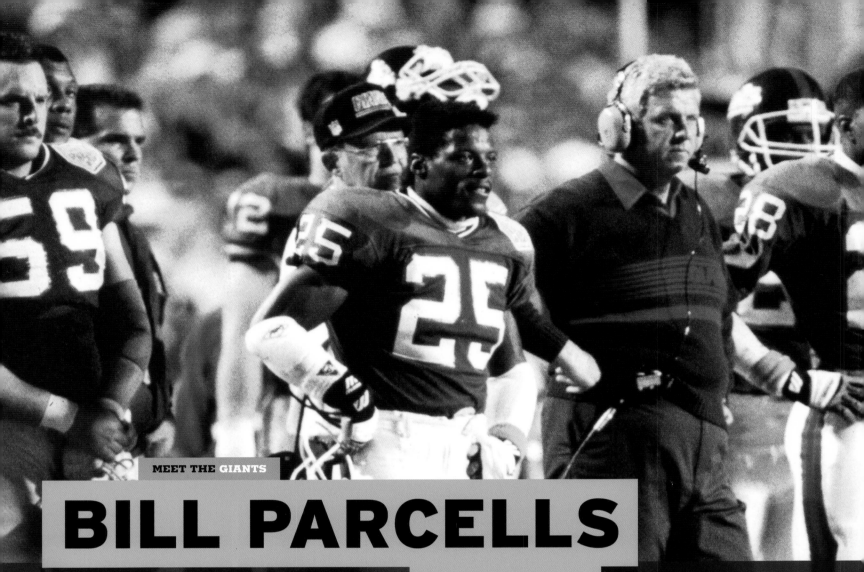

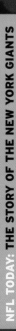

MEET THE GIANTS

BILL PARCELLS

COACH
GIANTS SEASONS: 1983-90

When he served as the Giants' head coach, Bill Parcells told his team, "There is winning, and there is misery."

Then he drove his players mercilessly to become winners. A typical Parcells practice session was like a war, and he was a loud, swearing general. Parcells was especially hard on his best players, such as Phil Simms and Lawrence Taylor. "You only yell at the people you trust," he once said. Parcells could be a tough taskmaster, but he was also a great motivator. "He took me, and he molded me, and he made me into a player," said Taylor. "My ability had something to do with that, but what Bill brought to the table was tremendous as far as I was concerned." During Parcells's 8 seasons running the Giants, his teams went a combined 77–49–1 in the regular season and assembled an 8–3 mark in the postseason. He was so intense that his health began to suffer, so Parcells retired after the Giants' 1990 Super Bowl win—but not for long. Three years later, he was back coaching and yelling at the New England Patriots.

hooked up with Burress for the winning score. "We shocked the world but not ourselves," linebacker Antonio Pierce.

Some experts thought New York's 2007 title was a fluke, but the 2008 Giants proved that they were the real deal by going 12–4 and running away with the NFC East crown. There would not be another Super Bowl parade in New York, however. Although the Giants had home-field advantage in the playoffs, they ran into a red-hot Eagles team in the second round and lost, 23–11.

The Giants, a team that entered the NFL as a $500 bargain more than 80 years ago, is today considered a priceless commodity by millions of football fans throughout the New York metropolitan area. Backed by decades of rich history and the enthusiastic support of the vocal New York faithful, today's Giants plan to continue making big news in America's biggest city for years to come.

Longtime Giants wideout Amani Toomer caught six passes to help New York pull off a monumental upset in Super Bowl XLII. **X**

INDEX

Anderson, Ottis 26

Barber, Tiki 31, 33, 39 , 40

Bavaro, Mark 26

Bradshaw, Ahmad 40

Brown, Roosevelt 17

Burress, Plaxico 40, 42, 47

Burt, Jim 35

Carson, Harry 35

Collins, Kerry 31

Conerly, Charlie 13, 17

conference championships 21

Coughlin, Tom 37, 39

Csonka, Larry 27

Danowski, Ed 13

division championships 13, 31, 47

"The Drive" 42, 43

Fassel, Jim 31, 37, 41

first season 10

Flaherty, Ray 12

Giants name 9

Giants Stadium 22, 31

Gifford, Frank 17, 21, 24

"The Greatest Game Ever Played" 17–18, 20

Haines, Henry 10

Hein, Mel 13, 15

Henry, Pete 10

Hilliard, Ike 37

Hostetler, Jeff 26

Howell, Jim Lee 14, 17, 18, 20

Hubbard, Cal 10

Huff, Sam 17

Jacobs, Brandon 40, 42

Johnson, Rob 21

Kanell, Danny 31

Leemans, Alphonse 13

Manning, Eli 37, 39, 40, 42, 43

Mara, Jack 24

Mara, Tim 9, 10, 11, 13

Mara, Wellington 15

McBride, Jack 10

Morris, Joe 25

MVP award 24, 25, 32, 36

NFC Championship Game 40

NFC championships 33

NFL Championship Game 12, 15, 18, 20, 21

NFL championships 10, 13, 15, 17, 26, 28, 47

Owen, Steve 10, 13, 14

Parcells, Bill 25, 26, 35, 37, 46

Pierce, Antonio 47

Pisarcik, Joe 27

Player of the Year award 17

playoffs 20, 25, 26, 33, 36, 40, 41, 47

Polo Grounds 9, 12

Pro Bowl 24, 32

Pro Football Hall of Fame 15, 17, 24, 32

retired number 36

Robustelli, Andy 17

Sherman, Allie 18

Shockey, Jeremy 34

Simms, Phil 22, 25, 26, 31, 32, 36, 46

"The Sneakers Game" 12

Strahan, Michael 31, 33, 40, 43

Summerall, Pat 20

Super Bowl 26, 28, 33, 35, 36, 40, 41, 42, 43, 46, 47

Super Bowl record 26

Tarkenton, Fran 21

Taylor, Lawrence 25, 31, 32, 36, 46

team records 24, 25, 36

Tittle, Y. A. 18, 21

Toomer, Amani 37, 40

Tucker, Bob 21

Tyree, David 42, 43

Umenyiora, Osi 43

Van Pelt, Brad 25

Warner, Kurt 39

Webster, Alex 17

Yankee Stadium 17, 20, 22

Young, George 22, 25